The
born
presenter

IAN MATTHEWS AND PAUL DAVIES

SKILLS PLEASE!

THOMSON
LEARNING ™

Australia • Canada • Mexico • Singapore • Spain • United Kingdom • United States

THOMSON

LEARNING

The born presenter

Copyright © Skills Please 2002

http://www.skillsplease.com

The Thomson Learning logo is a registered trademark used herein under licence.

For more information, contact Thomson Learning, Berkshire House, 168–173
High Holborn, London, WC1V 7AA or visit us on the World Wide Web at:
http://www.thomsonlearning.co.uk

British Library Cataloguing-in-Publication Data
A catalogue record for this book is available from the British Library

ISBN 1-86152-833-7

Text designed and typeset by **np**type, Lichfield, Staffs
Illustrations by Bill Piggins
Printed in Croata by Zrinski

Contents

Appendices

Foreword

Dear Presenter,

This book is designed to help both the novice and the experienced speaker. It contains three sections which can be used over and over again as a guide to any type of presentation, whether it is a sales pitch, report or briefing:

- In section 1 you will learn how to plan and prepare your presentation thoroughly;

- Section 2 contains power tips designed to help you to deliver your presentation with style;

- Finally, you will create your own presentation in section 3, using your unique Presentation Builder tool.

Remember, the art of creating and delivering a successful presentation is to keep it simple and stick to the basic principles involved. Presentations can be fun – so prepare diligently, act naturally and always maintain a sense of humour!

How to create your presentation

On completion of this section you will be able to:

 Plan and prepare your presentation venue

Confirm the purpose and type of presentation required

Identify your audience and their needs

Identify and organise your research material

Select and prepare a wide range of visual aids

Choose your oral delivery method

Planning your presentation

During a long presentation, most people within your audience will remain receptive for about 30-40 minutes. This time can be further broken down into a shorter attention span for each topic covered. You should not expect your audience to concentrate for longer than 10 minutes without a change of topic or delivery method. If your presentation is poorly constructed or difficult to follow, your audience will have difficulty concentrating for even 10 minutes!

You need a clear structure to your presentation, to enable the audience to follow its progression with ease. Even short presentations take a long time to prepare. Most business presentations or sales pitches are limited to between 10–20 minutes, which restricts your opportunity to include all of the important information and increases the preparation time required. One of the most universally accepted methods of planning your presentation is to use the SPAM model as a building block:

- Situation
- Purpose
- Audience
- Method

Let's take a look at each building block in turn:

Situation ■ Purpose ■ Audience ■ Method

- Check your venue
- Organise your schedule

Check your venue

In order to feel totally relaxed during your presentation, you must be completely familiar with the room facilities and layout. Where possible you should visit the chosen venue in advance, or talk to the facilities manager to thoroughly check arrangements. Use the following list to prepare yourself.

Your venue checklist *(Tick where applicable)*

☐ Do you know how long the presentation should last?

☐ Do you need to book the room?

☐ What is the start/finish time?

☐ Have you booked refreshments/lunch?

☐ What is the room size? – e.g. conference room, classroom or lecture hall.

☐ Will you need microphones/PA?

☐ Where are the doorways/fire exits?

☐ Are there any practice fire alarms scheduled/do you know where the assembly areas are?

☐ Where are the toilets/restroom/restaurant?

☐ Have you checked the heating/air conditioning? – Remember to set the temperature slightly cooler than is comfortable; a room becomes much warmer when it is full of people. If you make your audience too comfortable they will fall asleep!

☐ Are there adequate power sockets/will you need extension cables or overseas adaptors?

☐ Is the seating plan adequate? – Consider arranging the audience seats in a semi-circular pattern, as this is by far the best arrangement for acoustics and visibility.

☐ Have you tested the venue's presentation facilities? – If you intend to use any audio-visual equipment you must ensure that you are familiar with it. (See pp. 16–27)

☐ Is there adequate lighting? – Make sure you know how to dim the lights if required.

☐ Is your speaking area well lit?

☐ Are there windows/blinds? – Check that they operate correctly.

Organise your schedule

Your goal is to organise yourself, allowing you to concentrate on the presentation at hand. You should begin to prepare your presentation notes at least two weeks in advance. If your venue is not local, you must plan your travel and book your accommodation *immediately*. Always arrive at least an hour before your presentation, to give yourself plenty of time to prepare.

Finally, every experienced presenter has arrived at a venue to find that the equipment or materials which were booked in advance have not appeared. Always prepare for the worst scenario, travel with your 'Presenter's Survival Pack', containing enough essential materials to carry out a basic presentation given any circumstance:

The presenter's survival pack

- Nominal roll
- Slideshow – PowerPoint and/or 16mm
- Laptop
- Handouts/books
- Audience exercises/tests
- Notepads/audience pens
- Whiteboard marker pens
- Chalk
- Pre-prepared flip-chart – main headings
- Passport
- Credit cards

Your schedule checklist – *(Tick where applicable)*

☐ Have you confirmed your method of travel?

☐ Do you need to book rail/air tickets?

☐ Do you need to book hotel/accommodation?

☐ Have you packed all of your personal requirements, e.g. washing/shaving gear, clothing, alarm clock?

☐ Do you need to take any presentation equipment with you – e.g. projector?

☐ Do you have your presenter's survival pack?

☐ Do you have a route map to your hotel/venue?

☐ Have you got your passport/visa?

☐ How long will it take to get to your destination?

☐ Will you need to allow time to recover from jet-lag?

☐ Do you have enough spare cash or credit cards?

☐ Is your cash of the correct currency? – You may need some for taxis, restaurants etc.

☐ Have you contacted the venue organiser to confirm your arrival plans? – Check for contact numbers.

☐ Do you have a point of contact? – Phone number, e-mail address.

☐ Have you filled in your expenses form?

Situation ■ Purpose ■ Audience ■ Method

- Identify the aim/purpose
- Choose your topic

Identify the aim/purpose

You should always make every effort to deliver your presentation with the utmost enthusiasm. When choosing the purpose or type of presentation, first and foremost you must ensure that you tell the audience what they want to hear. There are three types of presentation:

- Informative
- Pursuasive
- Entertaining

Informative

In an informative presentation, the audience learns about a new topic or gathers more information about a familiar subject. Informative presentations can be delivered as a brief, a review or a report. The style of delivery could be an explanation, demonstration, description, or a series of actions or instructions. Whatever you present should contain a lot of information that is new to your audience.

Persuasive

A persuasive presentation is intended to change the audience's attitudes, opinions or behaviours, or to sell. All persuasive topics fall into one of four categories, depending upon the type of proposition or claim that you are making:

- An exploration of the worth of some idea or selling pitch

- A confidence building exercise

■ A recommendation of a specific course of action. This type of presentation is probably the most challenging because it is often about motivational or controversial subjects that are important to both speaker and audience.

■ Factual issues that usually involve conflicting evidence. The audience may be challenged or have to decide which statement is true or false.

Entertaining

If you are trying to entertain, do not expect your audience to be responsive if your delivery is dull and unimaginative! You want them to have a good time and to be amused or interested by the presentation, so try to gain and keep their attention using rapport, feedback and involvement. If you don't consider yourself to be naturally funny, use long jokes and stories sparingly!

Choose your topic

In most cases, the topic will have been decided for you, e.g. when you are presenting to a prospective employer, or delivering your company sales pitch to an external organisation.

Ask yourself:

- Does your topic address the audience needs?

- Will you enjoy talking about this topic?

- Will the audience be interested in your topic?

- Are you sure that topic won't offend some members of your audience?

- Does the occasion for your presentation have a special purpose?

- Do you know anything about the topic?

Your interest in the topic will also improve your ability to create the presentation, and it will increase your confidence when the time comes to present it.

Ideas seem to come automatically to presenters who have a topic in mind. Reference material that you read or discuss may suddenly relate to your topic and provide inspiration. The earlier you decide on a topic, the more you can take advantage of these coincidences.

Situation ◾ Purpose ◾ **Audience** ◾ Method

You arrive for a job interview. You have prepared a 20-minute presentation on a topic of your choice. As you walk into the location you are introduced to your future employer, who says …

'Hullo, Mr. Jones … I believe that you are giving us a presentation on ISO 9000 accreditation? What luck! I'm a qualified ISO 9000 assessor ….

A cold shiver runs down your spine, and then you begin to sweat …

One of the most important rules of any presentation is to know your audience. You must carry out prior research into the general background and level of knowledge of your audience. Try to obtain a nominal roll of those likely to attend, to determine their role within their company or organisation. You may even consider sending a questionnaire to all attendees, asking for any relevant information they would like to have included in the brief.

Your goal is to:

- ◾ Be perceived by the audience as credible and qualified to speak about your topic.
- ◾ Build a rapport with them and listen to what they have to say.
- ◾ Most importantly – ensure that the presentation *fulfils their needs*!

Your audience checklist

☐ What will they want to know, and what do they need to know?

☐ What is the size of the audience?

☐ What is the cultural make-up? – take care not to offend overseas visitors.

☐ Have you identified 'key' members of the audience?

☐ Do the members of the audience have anything in common?

☐ What will they already know about your topic?

☐ Will they leave the presentation well informed?

☐ What particular aspects of the topic will be most relevant to them?

☐ How can you involve the audience in your presentation – e.g. exercises/case studies.

☐ How can you best gain and hold their interest and attention? – e.g. quote real-life facts/examples or ask questions and opinions.

If possible, greet the audience as they arrive and chat to them. It is easier to deliver a presentation to a group of friends than to a group of strangers. Don't start your presentation with a 45-minute corporate video – it's a guaranteed turn-off! Include a self-introduction from all audience members – ask them what their expectations are or what they wish to gain from the presentation.

Other factors

The time of day could also have an affect on your audience:

■ Is the presentation immediately after lunch?

Listeners may need a hook, including some humour (be careful) or a startling introduction to gain their immediate attention.

■ Is the presentation late afternoon or evening?

People may be tired, therefore avoid any in-depth discussion or delivery.

■ Is the presentation on a Friday?

Involve and interact more with your audience to keep your listeners' minds from drifting to their weekend plans!

Situation ◼ Purpose ◼ Audience ◼ **Method**

- Organise your research material
- Select your audio/visual aids
- Choose your oral delivery

Organise your research material

There are many different sources that are available to you in order to research your topic. Do not be tempted to cover material with which *you* are familiar, but that bears no relevance to the audience's needs. Try not to include too much technical jargon or abbreviations, as not everyone will understand the latest buzzwords.

Resources

Your research methods should include:

The Internet

The Internet offers a wealth of resources, including popular search engines and newsgroups. You can search for relevant, up-to-date information on the web by simply entering keywords at popular search engines. Leading web sites for finding information on any topic include:

www.altavista.com
www.askjeeves.com
www.yahoo.com
www.about.com
www.google.com
www.excite.com
www.dogpile.com
www.amazon.com

Company intranet/literature

Most medium to large company organisations provide a local intranet, which can be a useful resource to gather internal news, product updates, and marketing information. You may wish to e-mail or call the IT helpdesk to assist you in your search.

Visit your local library

There are a few resources that are common to most libraries, including the library catalogue, reference works, newsletters and periodicals. You must, however, make sure that the research material is up to date. If you can't find exactly what you need, ask the librarian.

Personal networking skills

One of the most neglected but useful resources available to you is to ask work colleagues, friends, or family. You will usually find that these contacts are more than willing to help.

Collation

You should have a clear list of objectives which will set out what you wish to achieve with your presentation. Using these objectives you can start to organise your material. Organise your objectives to summarise the purpose of your presentation:

- The reason for the presentation;
- What the presentation will involve;
- What the benefits are to the audience.

Group similar themes and prioritise any facts, from the most to the least important. Begin to write and imagine that you are speaking the words to an audience. Keep your sentence construction as simple as possible, so that you will feel confident about the words you have to deliver.

It is perfectly acceptable to include light-hearted stories to add humour to your presentation. Real-life examples or anecdotes provide a useful break from your mainstream material and hence will enhance the enjoyment of your audience. One of the most popular methods of collating your material is to use the narrative methods of signposting.

- Tell them what you are going to say
- Tell them
- Tell them what you just said

Select your audio-visual aids

Presentations can be made far more effective by the correct use of audio-visual aids. Their primary function is to assist the understanding of the audience. In addition, good realistic aids add variety and make the presentation more interesting. Your goal is to give the audience direct sensory contact with your presentation, to improve knowledge retention.

Examples of visual aids

- People: Body, clothing, actions, gestures, voice, facial expressions and demeanour
- Sketches
- Pointer
- Handouts
- Graphs: Pie, bar, line
- Charts: Flow, tree, pictographs and flip.
- Photographs and pictures
- Posters
- Objects or models
- Audio-visual equipment:
    - Overhead projectors
    - Slides and transparencies
    - PowerPoint
- Handouts
- Films, videotapes, audiotapes, CD-ROM

Management of visual aids

When selecting a visual aid, the following points should be considered:

Relevant

Only select and use an aid if it makes the topic easier to understand. Avoid any unnecessary distractions and do not obscure the view of your audience. Remove or cover the visual aid when not in use.

Suitable

A readily available aid is not necessarily the most suitable aid. You must be imaginative. If you do not have the real thing, improvise using diagrams or models. You must prepare text and graphics with extreme diligence, as any spelling mistakes, inconsistent font sizes, wrong punctuation and errors will divert attention away from your presentation. Do not use models that are dirty, broken or unrepresentative of the real thing.

Entertaining

The use of colour, good layout, humour and realism will help to add interest.

Audible/visible

Aids must be seen or heard easily. Make sure that any slideshow projection is placed so that it fills the screen (and isn't crooked). Check for clear visibility by sitting in all locations in the room. Ensure that the volume of any audio equipment is set to acceptable levels.

Technique

When demonstrating aids, a useful three-stage technique is to TOUCH the aid, TURN to make eye contact with the audience, and then TALK to them.

Types of audio-visual aids

- PC/laptop and PowerPoint slideshow
- 16mm projector/slides
- TV/video
- OHP and transparencies
- Flipchart
- Whiteboard
- Microphone and PA system

Let's take a more detailed look at the most commonly used audio-visual aids:

PC/laptop and PowerPoint slideshow

The PC/laptop and digital projector is the most common form of audio-visual aid used today; however, it can also be the most complex. You should ensure that you are thoroughly familiar with any PC software, projector equipment or associated cables that you may be using.

Another commonly used visual aid is a slideshow. When used properly, a slideshow is a convincing aid to your presentation, but be careful not to overdo it. Most modern presenters seem to be more concerned with using the best computer visual effects rather than building a rapport with the audience. Be aware that people will not automatically be impressed by a state-of-the art animated computer image, especially if the content is confusing, illegible or contains grammatical errors. Many companies and educational establishments now have built-in video projectors and computers; as a consequence audiences are suffering from over exposure to identical clip arts and audio files.

PowerPoint is a very useful tool for the presenter; however the slideshow should be balanced and pleasing to the eye. As a general rule, keep it simple and relevant and avoid using too many slides or speeding up the presentation if you are behind schedule. A general rule of thumb to determine how many slides should be used during a presentation is:

- 10 minute presentation – one slide per minute.
- 40 minute presentation – one slide every 2 or 3 minutes.

Standard PowerPoint slide font sizes

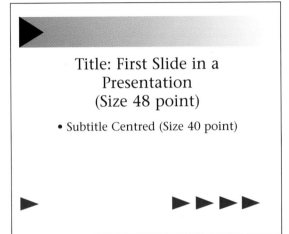
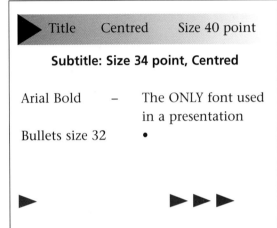

Note – some useful keyboard tips when using PowerPoint are displayed in Appendix 2.

Slide colours

The selection of slide and text colours is very important. Text and colours that look impressive on your laptop display may not be as legible on a larger screen. Try to limit your selection to a maximum of three colours. You must check your slide colour scheme using a large screen (preferably at the venue itself). You should also check that the slide detail is legible from all angles within the room.

Equipment checklist

- Is the PC/laptop connected to the projector/monitor?
- Do you need a power extension or any other connecting/adaptor cables?
- Has the PC/projector booted up correctly?
- Is the projector in focus?
- Does the slideshow run correctly?
- Are the slides clearly visible on the projection screen?
- Do you know how to use the remote control?
- Can you pause the slideshow or go back to earlier slides if asked?
- Do you have a back-up copy of your slideshow?

16mm carousel projector/slides

Although modern digital projectors are preferred over the 16mm version, some training establishments still use these to good effect. Many presenters have a 16mm back-up of their PowerPoint slideshow, in case of equipment failure.

Equipment checklist

- Test the equipment – is it functional?
- Is the projector in focus?
- Do you know how to use the remote control?
- Can you go back a slide if asked?
- Are the slides in the correct order?
- Are the slides numbered and the correct way up?
- Have you got blank slides if required?

TV/video

This is still a very popular audio-visual aid for the presenter. In most cases you may be using TV/video equipment which is unfamiliar to you, therefore you must check the equipment thoroughly. If you are not confident with its operation, seek out the facilities manager for assistance.

Equipment checklist

■ Test the equipment – is the video tuned into the TV?

■ Is the correct channel selected on the TV?

■ Do you know how to use the remote control?

■ Can the TV/monitor be clearly seen from all angles?

■ Is the volume set to acceptable levels?

OHP and transparencies

OHPs are notoriously difficult to position, so you must prepare them early. When you use transparencies make sure that you put them on the right way up and pile them neatly. Transparency frames can provide a useful place to write notes or key points to assist your delivery. To avoid distraction, when adding or removing transparencies switch the OHP off. Remember to turn it back on!

■ Does the OHP carry a spare bulb?

■ Test the equipment – can you position and focus the OHP onto the projection screen?

■ Have you remembered your transparencies?

■ Do you need any cleaning materials or wipes?

■ Do you have the correct marker pens?

■ Do you have different colours to highlight key points?

Flipchart

This is very easy to set up and can be found at most venues. You should always stand to one side when using a flipchart to ensure that your information is clearly visible. (Tip – Make sure that it's the side which gives you easy access to write with your *dominant* hand!).

Equipment checklist

■ Is there sufficient paper?

■ Do you have the correct marker pens?

■ Do you have different colour pens to highlight key points?

■ Are you sure that your writing is large and clear enough?

■ Do you need to prepare main headings in advance?

■ Write your name clearly on the page!

Whiteboard

Whiteboards are a very effective visual aid to your presentation. Information can be applied and removed quickly. However, you should ensure that you remove any information which is no longer relevant, so as to avoid distraction.

Equipment checklist

- Remember to wipe the board clean before you begin.
- Do you have a wiper/cleaning material?
- Do you have the correct whiteboard marker pens?
- Do you have different colour pens to highlight key points?
- Are you sure that your writing is large and clear enough?
- Have you cleaned the board after use?

Microphone and PA system

This audio accessory is now a common tool for the modern presenter when speaking to a medium or large size audience. When used correctly, the effect will help to project your voice, giving you more confidence. When using a clip-on microphone you should position it carefully (i.e., at chest height), as it may exaggerate noises such as breathing or sudden movements.

- Are the microphones, PA equipment and speakers serviceable?
- Does the equipment or cables pose any safety or electrical hazard?
- Can you be clearly heard from all angles of the room?
- Do you have a back-up hand-held microphone?

Choose your oral delivery

There are 3 main methods of oral delivery:

The narrative script – This is a full presentation script, built around three main headings: the beginning, a middle and an end. Your research material should be further subdivided into main points and should include examples or statistical facts. Highlight important sections using bold font, to help you with your delivery. You should edit this script until it sounds fluent in rehearsals. You may wish to annotate page and slide numbers within the script, if applicable. (See Section 3, Presentation Builder for further details)

Prompt cards/main headings – Using your full narrative script, you should extract the main points and jot them down on small pieces of card. These brief notes are designed to assist you if you lose your train of thought during the presentation. You may find it useful to highlight vital information in a different colour. Try to limit your information to three points per card and make sure that it is legible!

Speak from memory – This is not recommended unless you are an experienced presenter. You should memorise the entire presentation and if necessary, be prepared to ad lib to your audience. Most presenters tend to use an accompanying slideshow to prompt their oral delivery (and keep them on track!). When delivered successfully, these are the most impressive presentations, as it shows your audience that you have a complete mastery of your subject.

Most educational books encourage the presenter to abandon the narrative script and simply use prompt cards and main headings. In today's demanding workplace, however, you may not be given enough time to rehearse your presentation fully. Our recommendation is to use your narrative script until you feel confident enough to speak using either prompt cards or from memory. Your audience will appreciate a well-scripted delivery far more than any fumbled attempt to ad lib.

Summary ▪ Be prepared

For thorough preparation and planning you should apply the SPAM principles.

Test my understanding

You have been asked to give an important presentation for a large business organisation. To make sure that you are fully prepared, answer the following questions (answers are at the back of the book, in Appendix 3).

1 You have used the venue before. Do you:

a. Phone the venue's facilities manager to check that nothing has changed with regard to the rooms layout and facilities, prior to your presentation?

b. Arrange to check the room and facilities prior to your presentation?

c. Ask for a detailed diagram of the room layout to be sent to you by e-mail?

d. Because you are so busy, ask a colleague to check the venue and report back to you immediately?

2 To ensure that your presentation is relevant to the audiences needs, you should:

a. Use as many visual aids as possible.

b. Ensure that the presentation is delivered on-site at the customer's location.

c. Produce a list of objectives for the presentation.

d. Contact each member of the audience.

3 Your presentation topic is to be a progress review of your marketing strategy. What type of presentation should you use?

a. Entertaining

b. Informative

c. Persuasive

d. Aggressive

4 What is the most important factor in the successful delivery of a presentation?

a. Your presentation structure.

b. The research methods used.

c. Your audience.

d. Your experience.

5 Name three oral delivery methods.

6 What is the most important factor with regard to the presentation and your audience?

a. You must not include irrelevant information or slides.

b. What does your audience already know?

c. Who are the key members of the audience?

d. Does the presentation address the audiences needs?

7 List four audio-visual aid equipments you can use to assist your presentation.

8 Your slideshow presentation is to last 40 minutes. How many slides should be used?

a. One slide per 2–3 minutes

b. One slide per 4–5 minutes

c. One slide per 0–1 minutes

d. One slide per 5–7 minutes

9 You have discovered that some familiar faces will be present in the audience, therefore you intend to include some humorous slides, which may mean that you exceed your allocated presentation time. Do you:

a. Strongly agree with this statement?

b. Agree but postpone the decision to use the slides until the day?

c. Strongly disagree with this statement?

d. Contact the audience participants to verify if this is ok?

10 Name two methods that you can use to research your presentation material.

11 State the method used to correctly signpost your presentation.

How to deliver your presentation

On completion of this section you will be able to:

■ Overcome presentation fear and anxiety

■ Identify the quallties of a good presenter

■ Learn how to relax before your presentation

■ Cope with question and answer sessions

The qualities of a good presenter

Many people have to deliver a presentation, not because they want to, but purely by virtue of their appointment. They find themselves in a position where they have to get information across to other people – it could be for training, business, an interview or a project. Do you envy the qualities possessed by the 'born' presenter?

We don't wish to teach you to how become a clockwork presenter...however, there are certain CMADE qualities which you should strive for :

- **C**onfidence
- **M**anner
- **A**ttitude
- **D**iligence
- **E**nthusiasm

Let's look at each one in turn...

Confidence ■ Manner ■ Attitude ■ Diligence ■ Enthusiasm

This stems from a thorough knowledge of your subject matter, which you can only obtain through hard work and research:

■ You must know your topic, and your knowledge must be well above that of the audience.

■ Time is of vast importance – you *must* rehearse to ensure that you don't run over your allocated time. If possible, rehearse in front of an audience or colleague.

■ It is perfectly natural to feel nervous, especially before you begin your presentation. However, it is unlikely that your nerves are visible to the audience.

■ Use gestures appropriately when expressing emotions – but be sensible, too much gesturing can make you appear nervous.

■ If you are happy with your knowledge and secure in all of your planning, you should be confident of succeeding.

■ Remember, your success is going to breed even more confidence!

Confidence ◼ **Manner** ◼ Attitude ◼ Diligence ◼ Enthusiasm

The way you speak, move and your appearance during the presentation are extremely important. You should consider your:

◼ Vocal management
◼ Body management
◼ Personal appearance

Vocal management

◼ You should speak clearly and distinctly, using proper emphasis and avoiding a monotonous drone. Avoid reading every word displayed on the screen aloud – this shows a lack of in-depth knowledge.

◼ Use RSVP – vary the Rhythm, Speed, Volume and Pitch of your voice. This will help you to emphasise important points and keep the attention of the audience.

◼ To captivate the audience for a particular point, lean forwards and lower the tone of your voice.

If you have any doubts about the quality of your own voice, then you should record yourself on a tape recorder and play it back at home or in the car. Even better if you can video yourself!

◼ When using your vocals … RSVP If you please!

Body management

Eyes and face

Making eye contact will allow you to appear more approachable, gauge feedback and make the audience feel more involved.

◼ At every opportunity during your presentation, try to gain eye contact with members of your audience.

◼ Do not exclude anyone, make them all feel part of your presentation.

◼ Relax and smile, but remember – don't stare!

Stance/posture

- If you are standing still, try to adopt the 'A'-Stance; relax your shoulders and stand with your feet shoulder-width apart.

- A little normal movement adds a touch of variety to your presentation; but try not to move around the room continuously, as this is a distraction to the audience.

- Avoid crossing your arms – this will make you look less approachable.

- Hand gestures should be used to emphasise important points.

- Rehearse in front of a colleague or a mirror, to check for any unwanted mannerisms.

Personal appearance

- First impressions *do* count: your audience will be looking at you for most of the presentation.

- Your appearance should always be of a high standard.

- Consider tailoring your appearance to your audience.

- Oddities or scruffiness, lack of personal hygiene (e.g. sweaty armpits!) can prove distracting influences to the audience, and should be avoided.

- Always wear comfortable shoes, that don't squeak!

- Keep your hair manageable and tidy.

- Check yourself in a mirror before you start: a crooked tie is an unnecessary distraction.

Confidence ■ Manner ■ Attitude ■ Diligence ■ Enthusiasm

This largely depends on the type of presentation required – for example, informative, persuasive or entertaining. Follow the guidelines written below; with experience, you will be able to automatically tailor these guidelines as required.

- You must be *approachable* in all aspects. If you appear aggressive your audience will be reluctant to ask questions. Try to establish a presenter/audience rapport founded on mutual respect. It is your job to encourage class initiative, acknowledge student achievement, and make the class feel that their success really matters to you.

- You must be *fair*, avoiding favouritism with an individual, sarcasm or constantly selecting a weaker member of the audience to gain a cheap laugh. Avoid lying and where necessary admit mistakes – *never* bluff!

- You must keep control of your audience. You should be *firm*, so that they respond immediately to your lead and direction.

- You must be on *friendly* terms with the audience: however, avoid too much 'backslapping' and do not let them set the agenda.

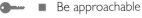

- Be approachable
- Be fair
- Be firm (if required)
- Be friendly

Confidence ◼ Manner ◼ Attitude ◼ # Diligence ◼ Enthusiasm

You must be painstaking and persistent in attention to detail, and should never cut corners at the expense of a good presentation. Never be satisfied with second-rate standards; the perfect presentation *does* exist! No matter how well you delivered your last presentation, always strive to improve.

- ◼ It's worth repeating – make your work legible and avoid spelling or grammatical errors. This is an unnecessary distraction.

- ◼ Never, never start your introduction on a negative note – For example:

> 'This is the first time I've done this….'
>
> 'I was caught in a traffic jam and I haven't quite woken up yet….'
>
> 'I don't usually give this presentation…'

These are all excuses for your lack of preparation and you have already lost the respect of your audience!

- ◼ Painstaking
- ◼ Persistent
- ◼ Attention to detail

Confidence ■ Manner ■ Attitude ■ Diligence ■ Enthusiasm

The dictionary defines 'enthusiasm' as 'intense interest, passionate zeal...'. This may sound a bit strong, but it is an essential quality in a presenter.

■ It is natural to appear enthusiastic about a very interesting subject. It follows that if you can retain your enthusiasm for a relatively dull subject, your drive and vigour will gain the audience's interest, and carry them along through the presentation.

■ You gain enthusiasm by a conviction of the importance of the subject matter, your rapport with the audience and by your confidence in your presentation skills.

Control your nerves

The minutes leading up to a presentation can be nerve-wracking. The good news is that over 40 per cent of people admit to having had some fear or anxiety when speaking in front of groups. People who have this fear can experience all kinds of symptoms; sweaty palms, accelerated heart rate, memory loss and even difficulty in breathing. Those presenters who lack self-confidence, or succumb to fear and anxiety during a presentation, should carry out the following procedures to control their nerves:

Prior to the presentation

■ Mentally rehearse your notes or your slideshow one last time;

■ Reassure yourself that you have planned thoroughly and your audience want you to succeed;

■ Write your name clearly on the flipchart/slide/whiteboard;

- Confirm your handling of any visual aids, remote controls or audio or video equipment;
- Stand at the lectern and speak into the room or microphone, to gauge the pitch and volume level required;
- Practise the 'impact' of your intro:
  1. Memorise it completely until it sounds relaxed and fluent;
  2. Start your presentation with an interesting statement or question;
  3. Practise it again!
- Walk around where the audience will be seated. Walk from where you will be seated to the place where you will be speaking;
- If possible, ensure that there is good ventilation in the room – a hot stuffy room can increase your anxiety;
- Try to anticipate and eliminate interruptions (fire alarms, mobile phones, cleaner, refreshment trolley etc);
- Place a sign on the door indicating that the room is occupied;
- Breathe deeply and smile!

During the presentation

- Establish initial eye contact with all of your audience;
- Make sure that your notes are clearly visible at all times;
- Try to think of your audience as individuals;
- Keep your introduction short – you do not want to begin with a stuttering, rambling intro!
- Try to deliver your first few minutes without looking at your script. Use your slideshow to prompt you;
- Do not to talk for longer than 40 minutes without giving your audience a coffee break. This will ensure that your audience remains receptive;
- Immediately after you call the break, relax and gather your thoughts for the next stage of your presentation;
- During the break, try to talk to members of the audience. This will make you appear more approachable and encourage participation on return to the presentation;

- On return, if you feel that the audience is unresponsive, interact by asking direct questions or opinions;
- Enjoy yourself!

Quick relaxation techniques

The moments leading up to your presentation are always tense – even for the experienced presenter. By following these simple exercises, you can help to relieve this tension and stay calm and relaxed. This series of relaxation techniques can be carried out almost anywhere and at any time, prior to your presentation. Just find yourself a quiet spot, close your eyes and treat yourself!

Breathing

Two-step breath – breathe in to fill the bottom of your lungs first, then fill the top of your lungs as you breathe in through your nose. Breathe out slowly. Feel the tension flowing out.

Tense-relax muscles

Tighten the muscle that you want to relax. Focus on this tension. Now let the muscle become loose and limp. Feel the relaxation flow into the muscle.

Body scan

With your mind, briefly concentrate on every muscle in your body, working from the tips of your toes to the top of your head. If you sense a tight muscle, imagine it becoming limp and relaxed.

Limp rag doll

- Do the two-step breath twice;
- Imagine that you are a rag doll. Feel your mind and body become limp and relaxed.

Relax your mind

To relax your mind, first focus on your breathing. As you breathe in say slowly to yourself '*I am*' and as you breathe out, say slowly '*relaxed*'. When your mind feels calm you should continue to focus purely on your breathing and nothing else.

How to cope with questions

The ability to cope with questions is one of the most useful skills for a presenter to master. Your goal is to be perceived by the audience as a credible presenter in order to gain their respect, and thus ensure that they remain alert and responsive. The best way to prepare for questions is to know your subject! However, since you can't always predict what you'll be asked, how can you prepare for the questioning?

In general, there are four types of questions which you may have to respond to:

- Relevant
- Irrelevant
- Don't know
- Hostile

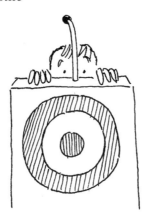

Here are a few guidelines:

Relevant

- Before you answer, take a moment to *reflect* on the question. By not rushing to give an answer, you show a degree of respect for the questioner and it will also help you to relax while you get your thoughts together.

■ If the person asking the question begins to ramble on, you should tactfully break into his flow and ask for clarification. Say something like 'If my understanding is correct, what you are asking is …'. This will focus the question and give you a place to begin an answer.

Irrelevant

■ If the question is a deliberate attempt to mislead, it should be dealt with politely, but firmly dismissed.

■ If the question is genuine but irrelevant, the presenter must deal with it constructively. As a general rule, do not dismiss the questioner, but don't waste valuable time.

Don't know

■ If you cannot answer the question, say so. Do *not* lie, bluff or apologise for being unable to answer. You should offer to research the answer to the question during a break – but remember to do it.

■ You could suggest resources (e.g. company brochures, books, the Internet) that would help the questioner to obtain the answer.

■ If you offer to follow-up with an answer at a later date, always get back to them – it will ensure that you (and your company's) image is preserved as a professional one.

Hostile

■ Be as honest as possible and your audience will support you.

■ If you are being heckled, try to maintain eye contact and stay calm.

■ Try to redirect hostile questions back to the audience.

■ If you feel confident enough, try to defuse the situation by telling a joke at your own expense.

- Give the questioner/heckler the opportunity to continue the discussion during a break or after the presentation.

- Avoid prolonged discussions with one person, extended answers, and especially arguments.

- Never let the heckler deter you from the flow of your presentation.

- In very extreme cases, and for the benefit of the remainder of your audience, ask the heckler to leave the room to calm down.

The seven-step handling technique

The most common method of handling questions is to:

1. Locate the person asking the question
2. Maintain eye contact and listen carefully to what is being asked
3. Wait for the questioner to finish talking
4. Break eye contact
5. *Repeat* or rephrase the question – a large audience may not have heard it and will 'switch off' if they don't feel involved.
6. Answer the question
7. Move on with the presentation.

Summary ▪ You've got it 'CMADE'!

You can gain *Confidence* in yourself by knowing your subject. With the right *Manner* and the correct *Attitude* you will gain a mutual respect with your audience. With your *Diligence* and your *Enthusiasm*, YOU now have the qualities required to be a first class presenter.

Test my understanding

Exercise 2

You have been asked to deliver a presentation for your company. Using your knowledge learned from this book, answer the following questions (answers are at the back of the book).

1 What is the most important factor in gaining confidence?

a. You are aware of the venue and timings

b. Your audience know little about your topic

c. You have a thorough knowledge of the topic or aim

d. You have found a presentation slideshow covering your topic

2 To ensure that you look relaxed, you should try to adopt the following posture:

a. The V stance

b. The B stance

c. The A stance

d. The D stance.

3 RSVP can be used for vocal management. What does it stand for?

R –

S –

V –

P -

4 What is the most important factor in the successful delivery of a presentation?

a. Your presentation structure

b. Your experience

c. The research methods used

d. Your audience.

5 Fill in the missing word:

In order to build a mutual respect and rapport with the audience, you must be _____.

6 What is the most important factor with regard to your diligence towards the presentation?

a. Never start the presentation on a negative note.

b. Make sure that there are no long sentences in your slideshow.

c. Check the seating plan and audience numbers.

d. Remember to pack up all equipment before you leave.

7 What does CMADE stand for?

8 Increased anxiety and drowsiness can normally be attributed to:

a. Too many visual aids

b. A hot stuffy room

c. Poor personal appearance

d. Not enough pens.

9 If an audience member asks an irrelevant question and begins to ramble on, how should you respond?

a. Ask a member of the audience to intervene

b. Stop the presentation and give the audience a break

c. Intervene and say 'that's enough – lets move on with the presentation'

d. Intervene and say ' If my understanding is correct, what you are asking is…'.

10 Fill in the missing word:

There are four types of question which can be asked, Relevant, Irrelevant, Don't Know and _____.

11 What is the maximum acceptable speaking time, without giving your audience a break?

Section 3

Presentation builder

On completion of this section you will be able to:

■ Create a detailed presentation narrative script

The Presentation Builder template

Introduction

The Presentation Builder design template will assist you to create your presentation in the form of a narrative script, with the help of an example scenario. Note that the template should not restrict your own ideas or any other relevant information that you feel could be useful. Each stage of the design template will consist of an example presentation, based on a given scenario. After each example, there is space provided to enter the details you require in order to create *your* actual presentation script. Once you have completed the template, you may wish to transfer your notes to the blank template in Appendix 1. The Presentation Builder template can be used over and over again, helping you to produce successful and memorable presentations.

The scenario

You are the personnel manager for the Salisbury Hotel. It is Friday afternoon and the hotel manager calls you by phone. He congratulates you on your recent recruitment programme and informs you that the new staff will need to be trained on hotel procedures as soon as possible. He suggests that you carry out a series of presentation briefs; the first should begin on Monday morning. You hastily agree – the manager bids you farewell, then hangs up the phone. It suddenly dawns on you that you have lost an opportunity to ask further questions!

You decide to gather your thoughts and read the book '*The Born Presenter*' for further inspiration. Two days later, you have used the SPAM principles to plan your presentation comprehensively. A brief summary of your plan concludes:

- The presentation will take place in the conference suite of the Salisbury Hotel.
- Your presentation topic is to focus on hotel policy and procedures.
- The audience will consist of four new staff members, the hotel manager, and the head chef.
- The presentation will last for 20 minutes.

Ready to create your presentation?…Do you have your pencil ready?…Let's go.

Presentation design template

There are two steps you must take to complete the template:

- Step 1 – calculate your presentation timings
- Step 2 – fill in your presentation content

Calculate your presentation timings

You should not actually need a watch or clock to keep within your presentation time limit. If you practise sufficiently you should get the timing spot on – however, always make sure that one is available. Be prepared to be flexible with your timings for the main parts of your presentation (e.g. you may wish to extend your introduction due to late arrivals) however *never* go over your overall allocated time! The percentage breakdowns of your presentation timings should be:

- The beginning (Introduction)   20%
- The middle (Core topic)   70%
- The end (Summary/conclusion)   10%

Note – these percentages should include time allocated for any questions!

Scenario – timings

Scenario title: *Hotel Procedures and Policy*

Presentation time: *20 mins*

Beginning: *4 mins*

Middle: *14 mins*

End: *2 mins*

Now enter *your* timings here

Your title:

Presentation time: ....*mins*

Beginning: ....*mins*

Middle:...........................*mins*

End:................................*mins*

Fill in your presentation content

Creating the content of your presentation can be compared to building a jigsaw – first you should make sure that you have all of the pieces, then put them all together to create a complete picture.

The beginning

- Self-introduction
- Preliminaries
- Aim/objective

The middle

- Main point one
- Main point two
- Maiin point three
- Main point four
- Confirmation (Q&A)

The end

- Summary/conclusion

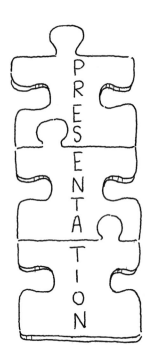

 The beginning

The beginning section of your presentation should consist of the following stages:

- Self-introduction
- Preliminaries
- Aim/objective of the presentation

Self-introduction

Your self-introduction should be kept brief. You should include:

- Your name
- Your role or background
- Your company's background

Scenario – self-introduction

'Good morning ladies and gentlemen, my name is Mike Riley. I'm the personnel manager of the Salisbury Hotel. Our hotel belongs to the Granada Trust chain of hotels, which, as you are aware, span the entire country.'

Your self-introduction

_____

_____

_____

_____

_____

_____

_____

_____

_____

_____

Preliminaries

Following your self-introduction, you should take the opportunity to make the audience aware of any administrative information that is relevant to the presentation. The following is a guideline to what you may wish to cover, if applicable:

- Roll call
- Do you need to mention any safety points? Fire drill/exits, trip hazards, first aid points, danger of electric shock, etc...
- Smoking (can/can't they)
- Lunch/coffee breaks
- Location of toilets
- Do they need to take notes? Are pens and paper provided?
- Are you supplying a précis? (if yes, tell them)
- Question procedure. Do you want them to stop you as you go through the presentation or keep all questions until the end?
- References to your presentation, e.g. books, policies, previous presentations, etc
- Any other information you perceive to be relevant.

Scenario – preliminaries

'Before we start I would just like to cover some preliminaries. First of all may I confirm everyone is here by taking a roll call of your names? You are all new to this building, therefore in the unlikely event of a fire may I ask you to proceed calmly through the door and follow the exit signs until you come to the front car park where you should all congregate. You may wish to take notes during this presentation, however there is an accompanying précis that you will be given later. Please do not hesitate to ask questions during suitable pauses. For your information, coffee and biscuits will be served during the refreshment break at half-past ten.'

Your – preliminaries

_____

_____

_____

_____

_____

_____

_____

_____

_____

Aim/objective

This should consist of short, sharp, clear statements. Where applicable, explain to your audience how they will benefit, both personally and as a group, from the information you are about to tell them.

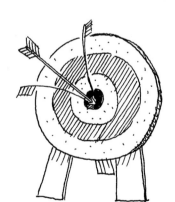

Scenario – aim/objective

'My aim today is to give you an overview of our hotel policy and working procedures. By the end of the presentation you will have a complete understanding of how the hotel is run, which will enable you to carry out your new roles efficiently.'

Your aim/objective

_____

_____

_____

_____

_____

_____

_____

_____

_____

_____

_____

The middle

You should now begin the middle section of your presentation by covering your core topic in depth. You should try to limit yourself to a maximum of four or five main points, however you may add more if required. Your main points should be concise and tell the audience what they will know by the end of the presentation. You can break down any points into sub-points to make the presentation easier to understand.

You should include a short question and answer session at the end of this part, to ensure that your audience have understood you.

Scenario – main points

'I intend to cover the hotel policy and procedures step by step, so that by the end of this presentation, you should be able to...

■ Give a brief outline of the history of the hotel;

■ Explain the organisational structure of the hotel. (I.e. Staff and departmental roles);

■ Be conversant with the hotel working procedures;

■ Understand where you fit in – your role.'

Your main points

■ _____

■ _____

■ _____

■ _____

■ _____

■ _____

■ _____

■ _____

■ _____

■ _____

■ _____

Scenario – first main point

■ (Give a brief outline of the history of the hotel)

'Let us first look at the history of the hotel. The Salisbury Hotel was built in 1893. For many years it provided accommodation for roughly 30–35 people, however in 1932 an additional annexe was built which...'

Your first main point

■ _____

_____

_____

_____

_____

_____

_____

_____

_____

_____

Your second main point

■ _____

_____

_____

_____

_____

_____

_____

_____

_____

_____

_____

Your third main point

■ _____

_____

_____

_____

_____

_____

_____

_____

_____

Your fourth main point

■ _____

_____

_____

_____

_____

_____

_____

_____

Create your remaining points on separate paper

Final Q&A

You should finish the middle section of your presentation with a final Q&A session:

- Questions to your audience – start by asking questions that are related to your core topic/main points.
- Questions from your audience – always finish your middle section by asking your audience if they have any questions on the whole of the presentation.

Note that there are occasions where questions *to* your audience are not required – use your discretion and apply them only where necessary.

Scenario – question(s) to

During my presentation, I covered the organisational structure of the hotel. I mentioned that it was a non-hierarchical structure of management. Can anyone tell me why this type of structure is of benefit to the running of a hotel?'

Your – question(s) to

_____

_____

_____

_____

_____

_____

_____

_____

_____

The end

The final section of your presentation is used to re-emphasise the key points of your presentation. Do not include new material and avoid going over the whole presentation again. Try to ensure that your audience are responsive by using a statement such as 'to summarise...'. Move to the front of the class for added impact and to focus your audience attention.

You should make every effort to finish in style, with short, sharp statements and an energetic and enthusiastic delivery – giving your audience something to remember you (and your company) by.

Scenario – summary/conclusion

'Ladies and gentlemen, to summarise: This hotel enjoys a proud history of providing quality service for our customers. The organisational structure consists of four departments: housekeeping, reception, bar/restaurant and the kitchen. The working practices of this hotel are designed to ensure that the comfort of the customer is paramount. You all have a vital role to play in our success. We are delighted to have you on board and I'm sure that you will all carry out your new roles professionally and with pride. Thank you and good luck!'

Your summary/conclusion

_____

_____

_____

_____

_____

_____

_____

_____

_____

_____

_____

_____

congratulations!

By completing this book you have now
created your own presentation script. We
recommend that you now transfer your
script onto the blank presentation
template shown in Appendix 1.

You have created a presentation script
built on a solid foundation of SPAM
planning principles. Coupled with a good
understanding of CMADE presentation
delivery skills, this should provide you with
the confidence you need to successfully
deliver your memorable presentation. Your
only remaining task is to remember that
having worked hard to plan your presentation, it's definitely worth taking the time to
rehearse thoroughly. You should never bluff it on the day – it could be your
credibility or your company's reputation that you are gambling with!

- ■ Try it
- ■ Test it
- ■ Time it
- ■ Rehearse it

Good Luck!

Blank presentation template

BEGINNING

_____

_____

_____

_____

_____

_____

_____

Self-introduction

_____

_____

_____

_____

_____

_____

_____

Prelims

_____

_____

_____

_____

_____

_____

Aim/objective

_____

_____

_____

_____

_____

_____

MIDDLE

_____

_____

_____

_____

_____

_____

_____

(Add more main points if required)

Main point 1

_____

_____

_____

_____

_____

_____

_____

_____

_____

Main point 2

_____

_____

_____

_____

_____

_____

_____

_____

Main point 3

_____

_____

_____

_____

_____

_____

_____

_____

Main point 4

_____

_____

_____

_____

_____

_____

_____

_____

Main point 5

_____

_____

_____

_____

_____

_____

_____

_____

Questions

_____

_____

_____

_____

_____

_____

_____

_____

END

_____

_____

_____

_____

_____

_____

_____

_____

Summary/conclusion

_____

_____

_____

_____

_____

_____

_____

_____

_____

PowerPoint tips

The following keystrokes can be used on your PC keyboard to control your PowerPoint slideshow using capital or lower case letters:

■ **To go to a specific slide number**
Type the slide number and press ENTER.

■ **To change the screen to black or white**
Press 'B' or 'W' respectively. Press them again to go back to the original slide show.

■ **To show or hide your pointer**
Press A or =

■ **To advance to the next slide**
Press mouse click or spacebar or 'N' or right arrow or down arrow or page down.

■ **To return to the previous slide**
Right mouse click or backspace or 'P' or left arrow or up arrow or page up.

■ **To end the show**
Press ESC or CTRL + the pause/break key to the right of the keyboard.

■ **To erase the screen annotations**
'E'

■ **To advance on mouse click**
'M'

■ **To advance to a hidden slide**
'H'

■ **To go back to slide 1**
Press and hold both mouse buttons down for two seconds.

Answers to exercises

Exercise 1

1.   b
2.   c
3.   b
4.   c
5.   Narrative script, prompt cards or main headings, memory.
6.   d
7.   Any four from OHP, flipchart, whiteboard, TV/video, PC/laptop, projector, microphone and PA system
8.   a
9.   c
10. Any two from Library, Internet, personal networking, company intranet.
11. Tell them what you are going to say – tell them – tell them what you just said

Exercise 2

1.   c
2.   c
3.   Rhythm, Speed, Volume, Pitch
4.   d
5.   Approachable
6.   a
7.   Confidence, Manner, Attitude, Diligence, Enthusiasm
8.   b
9.   d
10. Hostile
11. 40 minutes